D0522208

The Fireside Book

A picture and a poem
for every mood
chosen by

David Hope

Printed and Published by
D.C. THOMSON & CO., LTD.,
185 Fleet Street, LONDON EC4A 2HS.
© D.C. Thomson & Co., Ltd., 1992
ISBN 0 85116 550 8

A GIPSY LIFE

I WISH I were a gipsy
with a horse and caravan,
I'd eat my food beneath the stars
And be a happy man.

I'd wear a spotted neckerchief
And ear-rings made of gold,
My skin would be so tanned and tough
I'd never feel the cold.

A black-haired girl called Rosie
Would be my gipsy wife
And she'd share with me the pleasures
Of the gipsy way of life.

I'd leave the past behind me,
For it nothing much endears,
And the future would be something
Only seen 'twixt Dobbin's ears.

Clip-clopping round the country
Is the best way to explore
The ever-changing landscape
Where the view comes to your door.

No-one would be my master,
I'd be quite free to roam
And no matter where I travelled to
I'd always feel at home.

Elizabeth Bloomfield.

BESIDE LOCH ECK

SUN on the hills, a slow smile spreading
Over the contours of a weathered face.
Soft water-music spun on silver shale,
Broom, spread in vibrant fans of yellow lace
Upon the wide, green skirts edging the loch.
Wind through the pines, gentle as loving hands,
Leaf-whispers stirring in the stillness,
The breath of birds sighing where time expands
Into infinities of quietude.
Gorse, smouldering against the cool green slopes
Where drifts of bluebells mistily entwine
And seagulls lift and wheel like risen hopes
Above the realms of sun-warmed interlude.

Joan B. Howes

THE GARDEN

MY heart shall be thy garden. Come, my own,
Into thy garden; thine be happy hours
Among my fairest thoughts, my tallest flowers,
From root to crowning petal thine alone.
Thine is the place from where the seeds are sown
Up to the sky enclosed, with all its showers.
But ah, the birds, the birds! Who shall build bowers
To keep these thine? O friend, the birds have flown.

For as these come and go, and quit our pine
To follow the sweet season, or, newcomers,
Sing one song only from our alder-trees,
My heart has thoughts, which, though thine eyes hold mine,
Flit to the silent world and other summers,
With wings that dip beyond the silver seas.

Alice Meynell

'MENA

EVERY evening in the square,
  Up the street and down,
Hear the girl at No. 8
  Calling to the town:
" Philomena, 'Mena, 'Mena!
  'Mena, are you there?"
(Echo answers, " 'Mena, 'Mena,"
  All round the square.)

In her garden-walks at dusk
  'Mena hears the call,
Slowly bends and cleans herself
  Sitting on a wall.
" Philomena, 'Mena, 'Mena!
  'Mena, are you there?"
Philomena licks her paws
  And smooths down her hair.

The moon comes up behind the roofs;
  Still that voice is heard,
Like some singer in the street
  Or a late, lonely bird:
" Philomena, 'Mena, 'Mena!
  'Mena, are you there?"
Only echoes answering:
  The street is bare, is bare.

But when the lights go, one by one,
  And the moon is high,
Philomena's tail is seen
  Lifting to the sky.
" Philomena, 'Mena, 'Mena!
  Oh, you little pest!"
She rubs a leg, accepts her food,
  And settles down to rest.

Clive Sansom

THE WEATHERCOCK

SO high it strutted in the sun,
A man could see it plain,
From five miles off, a golden bird
Upon a glittering vane.

No common fowl; you'd swear it was
An eagle come to roost,
That once had clapped heraldic wings
In front of Caesar's host.

For who that had not seen it flee
Headlong before a gale,
Or veer when little puffs of wind
Put salt upon its tail,

Would ever dream such warlike boast
So vain a thing could be?
And golden crest and spurs but stand
For arch inconstancy?

O lovely traitor, where's the man
That does not long with you
To ride the heavens like a king
And changing, still be true?

Robin Wilson

W
N
S
E

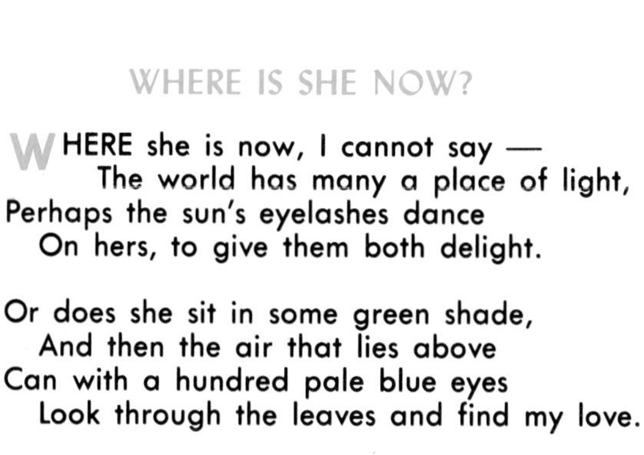

WHERE IS SHE NOW?

WHERE she is now, I cannot say —
The world has many a place of light,
Perhaps the sun's eyelashes dance
On hers, to give them both delight.

Or does she sit in some green shade,
And then the air that lies above
Can with a hundred pale blue eyes
Look through the leaves and find my love.

Perhaps she dreams of life with me,
Her cheek upon her finger-tips;
O that I could leap forward now,
Behind her back and, with my lips,

Break through those curls above her nape,
That hover close and lightly there;
To prove if they are substance, or
But shadows of her lovely hair.

W. H. Davies

THE HOUSE OF WINTER BLOSSOM

UP from the wild, exotic sea,
Up through the palm and the kapoc trees,
Along the trail of silver sand
The house of Winter blossom stands,
Bathed in the trade wind's timeless lore,
Echoing the ocean's roar.

Here the birds of olive noon,
Violet night and crimson dawn
Flash among the creaking sails
Of palms unleashed in balmy gales,
And the hotly-scented bower
Whispers mid the ocean's roar.

And sun from his eternal bower
Blossoms like a wondrous flower,
Blessing golden flower of moon,
Violet and temple bloom,
And from the wind-stung, breathless shore
The living sea's eternal roar.

And when the daytime cricket's ring
Softens, and the silent wings
From tree to tree through darkness blind
Swoop and circle, we will find
Our dreams in the gentle nights and pure
Imbued with a distant ocean's roar.

Eileen Melrose

AN OLD WOMAN OF THE ROADS

OH, to have a little house,
 To own the hearth and stool and all!
The heaped-up sods upon the fire,
 The pile of turf against the wall!

To have a clock with weights and chains
 And pendulum swinging up and down,
A dresser filled with shining delft,
 Speckled and white and blue and brown!

I could be busy all the day
 Clearing and sweeping hearth and floor,
And fixing on their shelf again
 My white and blue and speckled store!

I could be quiet there at night
 Beside the fire and by myself,
Sure of a bed, and loth to leave
 The ticking clock and the shining delft!

Och! but I'm weary of mist and dark,
 And roads where there's never a house or
 bush,
And tired I am of bog and road
 And the crying wind and the lonesome hush!

And I am praying to God on high,
 And I am praying Him night and day,
For a little house, a house of my own—
 Out of the wind's and the rain's way.

Padraic Colum

RHYME OF THE RAIL

SINGING through the forests, rattling over ridges,
Shooting under arches, rumbling over bridges,
Whizzing through the mountains, buzzing o'er the vale—
Bless me, this is pleasant, riding on the rail!

Men of different stations, in the eye of Fame,
Here are very quickly coming to the same;
High and lowly people, birds of every feather,
On a common level, travelling together!

Gentlemen in shorts, looming very tall;
Gentlemen at large, talking very small;
Gentlemen in tights, with a loose-ish mien;
Gentlemen in grey, looking rather green;

Gentlemen quite old, asking for the news;
Gentlemen in black, in a fit of blues;
Gentlemen in claret, sober as a vicar;
Gentlemen in tweed, dreadfully in liquor!

Woman with her baby, sitting *vis-à-vis;*
Baby keeps a-squalling, woman looks at me;
Asks about the distance; says it's tiresome talking,
Noises of the cars are so very shocking!

Singing through the forests, rattling over ridges,
Shooting under arches, rumbling over bridges,
Whizzing through the mountains, buzzing o'er the
vale—
Bless me, this is pleasant, riding on the rail!

J. G. Saxe

PLANTING TREES

TODAY six slender fruit trees stand
Where yesterday were none;
They have been planted by my hand,
And they shall dazzle in the sun
When all my Springs are done.

Two apples shall unfold their rose,
Two cherries their snow, two pears;
And fruit shall hang where blossom blows
When I am gone from these sweet airs
To where none knows or cares.

My heart is glad, my heart is high
With sudden ecstasy;
I have given back, before I die,
Some thanks for every lovely tree
That dead men grew for me.

V. H. Friedlaender

A SPRING SONNET

AGAIN on earth there is a rainbow born
    Brighter than arch a-kindle overhead—
The living warrant that old Winter's sped,
A song of wakening upon the morn.
Now bud-brake laughs; the elms are ruby red;
Pale emerald the coming of the corn;
And sunset lingers gold upon the thorn
Ere evening's violet counterpane be spread.

Where trust and hope on earth-born rainbows ring
Life with young April's fleeting fire and love,
While matin rose and silver wider fling
Their daily, dewy nets on hill and grove,
Each sunrise honours a new promise wove
Into the steadfast covenant of Spring.

Eden Phillpotts

NET LOSS

TIME was, my fishing net would land
  Ten tiddlers, easily one a minute;
But schoolboy skill forsakes my hand
And Father's net has nothing in it.

Eagerly my children wait,
Their jam-jars ready for the catch.
Alas! My skill they overrate . . .
Dad's met his piscatorial match.

Each fickle fin eludes my thrust,
And all I scoop is mud and stones.
My reputation's in the dust,
My prestige mourned with dismal moans,

"No fish? That boy's caught thousands, see!"
"And you — you haven't caught us any!"
And so, with all humility,
I seek this fishing prodigy
And buy some tiddlers . . . three a penny!

Noel Scott

ALL THE GOLD . . .

O MINE is the land of all the gold
Betwixt the sun and sea!
That golden land that shone of old,
That mountain land so golden bold,
It shines each hour for me.

That mountain land, that shining land:
Tho' but a rood I've won,
More wealth is mine than Asian sand,
With all the grains of every strand
Betwixt the sea and sun.

That golden country undefiled,
Those valleys rich and free,
Those mountain tops so golden wild:
Mine is this kingdom shining-piled,
Brighter than sun or sea.

Nina Cust

THE BALLIOL ROOKS

THE Winter is dead, and the Spring is a-dying,
And Summer is marching o'er mountain and plain,
And tossing and tumbling and calling and crying
The Balliol rooks are above us again;
And watching them wheel on unwearied wings,
I question them softly of vanished things.

O rooks, have you leant from your heights and harkened
From year to year to the whirl below?
While the suns have flamed and the days have darkened,
Have you marked men ceaselessly come and go,
Loiter a little while here and pass
As the ripple on water, the shadow on grass—

The monk with his orisons heavenward rolling,
The friar of black, and the friar of grey;
The schoolman stern, and the cavalier trolling
In court and in cloister his roundelay,
The singer sweet and the preacher pale —
O rooks, can you tell me their wondrous tale?

And they that shall follow upon us hereafter,
The men unknown of the unborn years,
Will they move you at all with their grief and laughter,
Will you reck, oh rooks, of their hopes and fears;
Or will you but circle scornfully,
And mock at them as you mock at me?

Frederick S. Boas

B.Glebska

IN HER GARDEN

IN her garden once, at a Summer noon,
Back in the shade I sat adream,
Oh, deep in the past where happiness
Was near and bountiful as the gleam
Of sun on the path; and ever too soon
Did the roses fade and the Summer go,
And daylight wane to the stars and moon,
And love was a cloak to Winter's stress
In the ways of our life so long ago . . .

Sudden I woke — alert — and bent,
Breathless, eyes and soul aware,
Watching — watching — all intent
On the straggling crimson rose that leant
Over the bed and border where
The path came round to my sheltered nook . . .
Was she on the path beyond the tree?
Had I heart to dare? Had I eyes to see?
Should I stay — or steal to the bend and look?
Ah, God, was she coming — coming to me?

No foot on the path, no voice, no face,
Not a stirring leaf where the roses bent
Over the path to the sheltered place
Where I sat afraid to leap to her.
Longing — knowing — I waited intent . . .
And she never came . . .
But she was there!

Shan Bullock

HARBOUR LIGHTS

I'VE travelled through Arabia,
  And even far Cathay,
I've gazed on holy temples,
  And trod the Pilgrim's Way.

I've sailed to South Sea islands,
  Trekked all through Nepal,
Panned for gold in the Klondyke,
  Hunted tigers in Bengal.

I've climbed high snow-capped mountains,
  Run the rapids to their end,
Found friendship and adventure,
  Round every blessed bend.

I've tramped the wide world over,
  But no matter where I roam,
The finest sight I'll ever see
  Are the harbour lights of home!

Glenda Moore

MOUNTAIN JOURNEY

GO well, adventurous day, and bravely run
From moonset to the echoing afterglow,
With burning accolade of mountain sun
And icy whine of wind across the snow;
While on the rope, unseen companions go —
Brotherly love, and fear that purifies —
And life and death, near neighbours in the skies,
Ponder the littleness of earth below.

And after, in the fretful street no less
Than on the pure and perilous verge of space,
We still shall keep for comfort in distress
The freedom of this high and shining place;
And still our fevered hearts may seek release
In distant snows, and there regain their peace.

Audrey Field

HIGH SUMMER

SHIMMER of sunbeams on bright water,
Glimmer of daisies, scent of hay,
Church bells chiming — oh, so softly,
Over the fields, from far away.
Dabble of ducklings on the river,
Downy and golden, drifting by,
Willows, with pale green, tossing tresses,
Under the bluest-ever sky.
Murmur of wild doves in the coppice,
Laughter of children at their play,
Oh, this is Summer in all its glory,
This is a perfect Summer's day!

Kathleen O'Farrell

WISHES FOR WILLIAM

THESE things I wish you for our friendship's sake
— A sunburnt thatch, a door to face the sun
At westering, the noise of homing rooks,
A kind, old, lazy chair, a courtly cat
To rub against your knees,
Shelves of well-chosen books —
I wish you these.

I wish you friends whose wisdom makes them kind,
Well-leisured friends to share your evening's peace,
Friends who can season knowledge with a laugh.
A hedge of lavender, a patch of thyme,
With sage and marjoram and rosemary,
A damask rosebush and a hive of bees,
And cabbages that hold the morning dew,
A blackbird in the orchard boughs — all these
And — God bless you.

Children, no matter whose, to wait for you
With flower faces at your garden gate,
And one to watch the clock with eager eyes,
Saying, "He's late — he's late!"

W. M. Letts

POINT OF VIEW

AGAINST my window stands a tree,
The tree is tall, my window high;
So I look up, or look I down,
Seeking a glimpse of April sky,
Or primroses abloom maybe,
I peer through branches swelling brown
That only change with sun and rain,
When blustering west winds toss and sway,
Or twilight droops to peace again,
And magic Spring breathes fuller strain
Among the buds day after day.

We two are friends, the tree and I,
Both of a height, and age perchance,
I talk to it and it to me,
Or greet with casual nod and glance,
And so keep heart and company.
"Ah, well for you," it says to me,
"Secure from rain and frost and blight,
From clinging mist and torturing wind,
The fickle day, the long drawn night:
Lone, rooted, helpless, such my plight,
Year after year and years behind."

"Keep heart, my friend," I answer then,
"The north wind brings you doleful mood.
You'll cheer when in a week or two
You get the Springtide in your blood
And swell to scorn of puny men.
Clean, strong your life, God-favoured, you
Toil not nor sow, yet bounties reap
Of freedom, beauty, communing
With stars and birds and dawn and sleep.
We wane and pass. You ageless keep,
Waxing, renewing, Spring by Spring."

Shan Bullock

TWO OLD MEN

TWO old men hailed me
as I went walking,
and we were talking
Of lovely things—
The glint of the sun on a moorcock's feather,
The lilt of the song the maiden sings
When she herds her cattle on Beinn-na-Caillich,
And how the peat-reek rises blue:
And och, but my heart was loving, loving
The youngest old men I ever knew!

Two old men hailed me
as I went walking,
and we were talking
The hours away:
Talking of island rune and blessing,
Of fairy piping on Cruachan grey.
And we were saying how God in Heaven
Paints dark Loch Leven so deeply blue;
And och, and och, but my heart was loving
The kindest old men I ever knew!

I'm saying a prayer
as I go walking,
softly talking
To God on high;
That He Who orders the moorland breezes,
The track of the sun across the sky,
May guide and guard, wherever they wander,
My two old friends the long day through:
For och, but my heart is always loving
The dearest old men I ever knew!

Sydney Bell

THE WAY TO ERICSTANE

'TIS on the way to Ericstane that ragged robins blow
Among the windy grasses by the hedge,
And far beyond those quiet fields the Annan waters flow
Where ripples rustle to the reedy sedge.

Oh, the road is rough and narrow on the way to Ericstane,
And the path's a weary path to tread alone;
But it's there I would be tramping to the purple hills again
In the dusk-hour when the summer day is gone.

Come, there the hills are dreaming and the veils of twilight fall,
The weary winds are dying o'er the fern,
And there's one who waits to claim you where the river-voices call
Through the dewy dusk beside the little burn.

A shade, among the shadows, he comes as long ago;
He came to greet us in the eventide,
His eyes are full of pity, his voice is soft and low
As the wind that wanders by the waterside.

He will fold us to the mountains, he has waited while we strayed
Through the mountains of the world to come again
From our pilgrimage triumphant and with spirit unafraid
To our Father hills that circle Ericstane.

Joan Rundall

FAMILY LIFE

PLEASE take me trout fishing, Daddy,"
The eager young angler said.

"Our best prospect will be that pool by the mill,
But at noontide the water is dead.
So I'll help you cast flies at the evening rise
After your sister's in bed."

"Show me a wild deer, Daddy,"
The nine year old naturalist said.
"A stag with big horns, or a doe with her fawns!"

"Through the woodland we'll noiselessly tread:
So give me a shake at the crack of daybreak,
Leaving your brother in bed."

At breakfast the following morning,
The youngsters excitedly fed.
He told of their sport, and the fish that he caught,
As the rings on the still water spread.
The whole of *her* talk was of sights on their walk —
A roebuck, with coat foxy red;
While their ghillie and guide, though rejoicing inside,
Was wearily nodding his head!

George Darwall

A COUNTRY CHURCHYARD

A GOLDEN moon rides high
On his road of hyacinth:
Black-shelved against the sky
The deep-boughed cedars sigh,
As a little wind goes by
Smelling of thyme and mint.

High on the cedared wall
The milk-white peacock stands,
Staid in his cedar stall,
Ivory-tailed and tall,
Calling his magic call,
Telling of magic lands.

Full in the moonbeam's path
The milk-white lilacs bloom,
Wreath upon incensed wreath,
Scenting with magic breath,
Steeping the field of death
In Eden-sweet perfume.

Thick on the moon-lit ground
The glimmering gravestones show,
Mound by shadowy mound,
Deep in earth's fragrance drowned,
Heedless of stir or sound,
The white bones sleep below.

Nina Cust

A MALVERN LYRIC

COOL where the clean winds travel
Along the solemn hills,
We watch the flowing splendour
That Summer brews and spills
From Malvern down to Bredon
Across the mellow plain,
Transfiguring the lowlands
Of shining leaves and grain.

Above the black pine-shadows
We dream beneath the sky,
And watch the far-flung valleys
Of Severn and of Wye,
And see the white clouds, walking
The great blue road that spans
The world from Wales to Cotswold,
Like ghostly caravans.

From beacon on to beacon,
  From shire to burning shire
The full day flames triumphant
  All girt in golden fire,
And here above the meadows
  Fire-garmented and shod,
We find a little haven
  Among the winds of God.

John Drinkwater

GOLDEN HOURS

MAKE me a garden, love of mine,
Of hollyhocks and columbine,
With lavender to scent the air
And honeysuckle everywhere,
Let roses trail along the wall,
Beneath them violets, pansies, all
Our childhood flowers.

Plant primroses and ladies' pride
Where lilac blossoms, side by side,
Hang over sunny bowers,
And there we'll sit when we grow old,
Content to see the years unfold,
As we tell tales we've oftimes told
And share our precious golden hours.

D.J. Morris

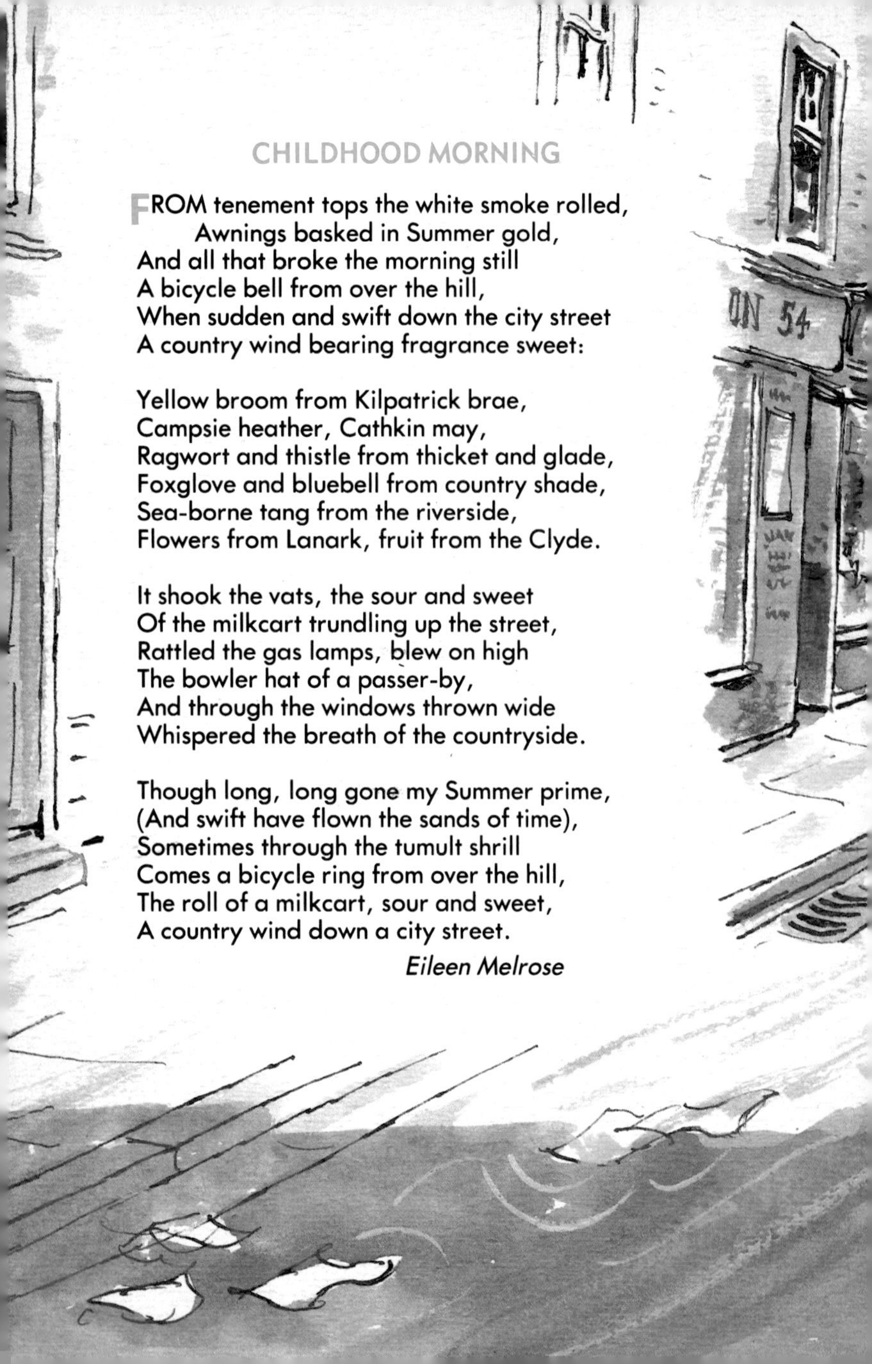

CHILDHOOD MORNING

FROM tenement tops the white smoke rolled,
    Awnings basked in Summer gold,
And all that broke the morning still
A bicycle bell from over the hill,
When sudden and swift down the city street
A country wind bearing fragrance sweet:

Yellow broom from Kilpatrick brae,
Campsie heather, Cathkin may,
Ragwort and thistle from thicket and glade,
Foxglove and bluebell from country shade,
Sea-borne tang from the riverside,
Flowers from Lanark, fruit from the Clyde.

It shook the vats, the sour and sweet
Of the milkcart trundling up the street,
Rattled the gas lamps, blew on high
The bowler hat of a passer-by,
And through the windows thrown wide
Whispered the breath of the countryside.

Though long, long gone my Summer prime,
(And swift have flown the sands of time),
Sometimes through the tumult shrill
Comes a bicycle ring from over the hill,
The roll of a milkcart, sour and sweet,
A country wind down a city street.

Eileen Melrose

WATSONS

DONEGAL COAST

I KNOW that at the end,
obedient to the sea,
I shall come
to this last utter coast
blinded with light.

All colour gone
but the swift spate of silver,
the grey mountain-shoulder,
wave-commanding,
and my hope in its fastness!

Divided, forsaken,
what should I cling to?
Thought, memory,
the nets of religion
break like a shoal in the sundering tide-streams.

Here, then, I stand
as night before morning,
the sea at dawn
and the long waves breaking;
O bright, Homeric waters
I pray you receive me.

Not as a stranger,
not as an outcast,
I come as thy pilgrim
I call thee to claim me,
by the sands on my feet
by the salt in my heart.

Robin Wilson

SOME DAY

THERE'S a land of hill and forest
Rolling westward to the sea;
I'm waiting for the day when you
Will ride that land with me.
The charm of fern and waterfall,
The far-flung moorland wide,
Are calling me to come; but you
Will travel at my side.

I'll show you lonely spaces
Where the swooping curlew cry;
A kingdom where the buzzard hawk
Aloft can cruise the sky;
Where deer are lurking in the glades,
And dappled sunlight plays
Through lacing branches overhead
Along the leafy ways.

I've seen the hills at sunrise
Dark against the eastern gold,
And travelled 'neath a sunset sky
Until the stars were cold.
A day will come when, with the far
Horizon as our guide,
Away, beyond the distant ridge,
Together we shall ride.

Iris M. Raikes

STORM WARNING

RED the small port light is blinking,
Distracted gulls insanely wheel,
Clinking sailboats waving, tossing
Into skies of wind-torn steel.

Close the trawlers crowd and riding
High on choppy harbour sea,
Spindrift over walls, waves rising
In wild unfettered symphony.

Crouching trees and birds in hiding,
Rain like gunfire on the pane,
Time to batten down the hatches,
The weather forecast — "Hurricane!"

Kathryn L. Garrod

ALL GONE

THE Grindstone Man is gone, with his singing
grindstone.
— *Sing, Grindstone, a rusty sad farewell.*
His rusty beard and rusty wheel are gone now,
No more his foot treads out that screaming music,
No more the water drips,
Nor lean knife slips
Upon the shrieking wheel; the Grindstone Man is
gone.

The Muffin Man is gone, with his evening bell.
— *Ring clear bell, a childish sweet farewell.*
His green baize apron and his padded coronet
Are wanting now, and coffin-like long tray.
No more the bell's clear ringing,
The cry of "Muffins!" singing
In brief November dusk: the Muffin Man is gone.

And Punch and Judy are gone, with the crimson
booth.
— *Whine again, sad Toby, your hungry last
farewell.*
The staff and cap and bells and all are gone now,
No more is heard gruff threat and squeaky cry;
No more the nodding heads,
And cap with gilded threads —
Even Punch and Judy and Toby and all are gone.

John Freeman

ON THE SUSSEX DOWNS

OVER the downs there were birds flying,
  Far off glittered the sea,
And toward the north the weald of Sussex
  Lay like a kingdom under me.

I was happier than the larks
  That nest on the downs and sing to the sky,
Over the downs the birds flying
  Were not so happy as I.

It was not you, though you were near,
  Though you were good to hear and see,
It was not earth, it was not heaven,
  It was myself that sang in me.

Sara Teasdale

BEN

WALK softly past the glowing tree of Heaven,
For here Ben sleeps,
Where he would most have wished,
Within the quiet garden of School House,
The glad, familiar sounds of every day —
Footfall, birdcall, the rush of wind through
leaves —
Lulling his long dream with sheltered ease.

The kindly trees beyond the weathered fence
Sing befitting elegies.
One tiny cypress on his resting place —
A small green candle set with gentle care
To point his way
To the warm certitude in which he lies,
Among the petal dust of memories.

Joan B. Howes

BOOKWORM

FAR in the past I peer, and see
  A child upon the nursery floor,
A child with books upon his knee,
Who asks, like Oliver, for more!
The number of his years is four,
And yet in letters hath he skill,
How deep he dives in fairy-lore!
The books I loved, I love them still.

One gift the fairies gave me (three
They commonly bestowed of yore):
The love of books, the golden key
That opens the enchanted door;
Behind it Bluebeard lurks, and o'er
And o'er doth Jack his giants kill,
And there is all Aladdin's store —
The books I loved, I love them still.

Take all, but leave my books to me!
These heavy creels of old we bore
We fill not now, nor wander free,
Nor wear the heart that once we wore;
Not now each river seems to pour
His waters from the Muses' hill;
Though something's gone from stream and shore,
The books I loved, I love them still.

Fate, that art Queen by shore and sea,
We bow submissive to thy will,
Ah, grant, by some benign decree,
The books I loved — to love them still.

Andrew Lang

ON THE RIVER

O SWEET Spring days!
Upon the shining reaches of the river,
When April dances down the flowery ways
Above the fens where scented breezes shiver:
O sweet Spring days!

Dream-golden days!
When on soft banks faint hawthorns pale and quiver
And drowsy sweet, the slow bough softly sways
Above the silent reaches of the river:
Dream-golden days!

Dear far-off days!
Adown the rippling reaches of the river,
Deep in my wandering heart their sweetness stays:
Ah! fade ye may, but ye can leave me never,
Dear far-off days!

Through golden days
Could we, adown the reaches of life's river,
Glide on, dear love, to parting of the ways,
Then kiss farewell — and meet to see for ever
Heaven's golden days!

Herbert Kennedy

brave
lament
peoples wrongs

THE LOVE SONG

"HERE lies a maker of golden songs,
Who sang for the beautiful and the brave,
And made lament for his people's wrongs."
And the wind's a-whistle about his grave.

But many waters quench not love!
This much remains of that nameless Bard:
One love-song, sweet as the lark's above,
One raindrop saved from the broken shard.

"Beloved, when our hearts are one
For ever in the dreamless dust,
And feel no more beneath the sun
Sweet pain of love's defendless thrust;

"My song for evermore shall tell
The legend of your dear regard;
And bear ev'n to the lip of Hell
This raindrop from love's broken shard!"

Malcolm K. MacMillan

A SONG OF GLOUCESTERSHIRE

NORTH, South, East and West:
Think of whichever you love the best.
Forest and vale and high blue hill:
You may have whichever you will,
And quaff one cup to the love o' your soul
Before we drink to the lovely whole.

Here are high hills with towns all stone,
(Did you come from the Cotswolds then?)
And an architecture all their own,
And a breed of sturdy men.

But here's a forest old and stern,
(Say, do you know the Wye?)
Where sunlight dapples green miles of fern,
A river wandering by.

Here's peaceful meadowland and kine,
(Do you see a fair grey tower?)
Where sweet together close entwine
Grass, clover, and daisy flower.

Here stretches the land towards the sea
(Behold the castle bold!)
Where men live out life merrily,
And die merry and old.

North, South, East and West:
Think of whichever you love the best.
Forest and vale and high blue hill:
You may have whichever you will,
And quaff one cup to the love o' your soul
Before we drink to the lovely whole.

F. W. Harvey

BLUE CHINA

THERE'S a joy without canker or cark,
There's a pleasure eternally new,
'Tis to gloat on the glaze and the mark
Of china that's ancient and blue;
Unchipped all the centuries through
It has passed, since the chime of it rang,
And they fashioned it, figure and hue,
In the reign of the Emperor Hwang.

These dragons (their tails, you remark,
Into bunches of gillyflowers grew),
When Noah came out of the ark,
Did these lie in wait for his crew?
They snorted, they snapped, and they slew,
They were mighty of fin and of fang,
And their portraits Celestials drew
In the reign of the Emperor Hwang.

Here's a pot with a cot in a park,
In a park where the peach-blossoms blew,
Where the lovers eloped in the dark,
Lived, died, and were changed into two
Bright birds that eternally flew
Through the boughs of the may, as they sang;
'Tis a tale was undoubtedly true
In the reign of the Emperor Hwang.

Come, snarl at my ecstasies, do,
Kind critic, your "tongue has a tang",
But a sage never heeded a shrew
In the reign of the Emperor Hwang.

Andrew Lang

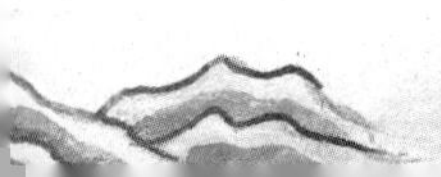

WOULD YOU RETURN?

POPPIES never brighter shone, and never sweeter smelled the hay,
The town with its steeples looked made of silver all the way,
Down in the streamy valley like a treasure that town lay.

Who was not with me there? Who in that crystal air
Hastened not beside me on the shorn baulk, did not stare
Miles ahead where those bright tops of mansioned hope were gems aflare?

Come then, know again this same knoll we paused upon,
These poplars with their flashing wind, this singing mill, this silent stone —
The sun pale peering at the shag-haired storm that swooped on Avalon!

Edmund Blunden

LAST OF THE SAILS

ONCE she wandered, a tawny vagrant, mistress
and slave of the fickle breeze,
Where the wind of the west was fragrant with the
heather's breath and the sea's.
But memory fades, and beauty perishes; all things
lovely under the moon
And the things the heart most cherishes, pass for
ever and pass most soon.

Pride she was of the old sea's children; dear she was
to the old sea's heart,
She alone on his dim horizon rests, while all of his
loves depart
Past the lee of the utmost islands, where the cries of
the sea-birds cease,
Sail and spar through the silver silence, pilgrims
passing into peace.

Malcolm K. MacMillan

WINE AND WATER

OLD Noah he had an ostrich farm and fowls on the largest scale,
He ate his egg with a ladle in an egg-cup big as a pail,
And the soup he took was elephant soup and the fish he took was whale,
But they all were small to the cellar he took when he set out to sail,
And Noah he often said to his wife when he sat down to dine,
"I don't care where the water goes if it doesn't get into the wine."

The cataract of the cliff of heaven fell blinding off the brink
As if it would wash the stars away as suds go down a sink,
The seven heavens came roaring down for the throats of hell to drink,
And Noah he cocked his eye and said, "It looks like rain, I think,
The water has drowned the Matterhorn as deep as a Mendip mine,
But I don't care where the water goes if it doesn't get into the wine."

But Noah he sinned, and we have sinned; on tipsy feet we trod,
Till a great big black teetotaller was sent to us for a rod,
And you can't get wine at a P.S.A., or chapel, or Eisteddfod,
For the curse of water has come again because of the wrath of God,
And water is on the Bishop's board and the Higher Thinker's shrine,
But I don't care where the water goes if it doesn't get into the wine!

G. K. Chesterton

THE VOICE

COLD was the church and grey:
  Cold the dim arches in the tremulous gloom:
Outside on pavements where the sun had lain
Shuddering from far away,
Like dead, white fingers tapping on a tomb,
The pitiless song of the cold Autumn rain!

Dark! Not a movement stirs
The silent throng of worshippers.
Slow, solemn voices steal across the dark,
Sullenly thrills the organ's trembling tone;
There on the altar a lamp burns — one spark
Twinkling uncertainly afar.
Dark: and my soul feels deadened and alone —
Lost in the night without one guiding star.

Then up aloft, one voice, a boy's clear singing —
Singing his soul out — up and out and away —
Far from this earth, on wings of angels, bringing
Tears to my eyes, peace to my heart, and joy
Perfect amid this life's imperfect day:
Freeing my soul of a chain —
Out from the gloom and the darkness again,
Outward and upward to God, and — only the
  voice of a boy!

Herbert Kennedy

THE FIELDMOUSE

WHERE the acorn tumbles down,
Where the ash tree sheds its berry,
With your fur so soft and brown,
With your eyes so round and merry,
Scarcely moving the long grass,
Fieldmouse, I can see you pass.

Little thing, in what dark den,
Lie you all the winter sleeping?
Till warm weather comes again,
Then once more I see you peeping
Round about the tall tree roots,
Nibbling at their fallen fruits.

Fieldmouse, fieldmouse, do not go
Where the farmer stacks his treasure,
Find the nut that falls below,
Eat the acorn at your pleasure,
But you must not steal the grain
He has stacked with so much pain.

Make your hole where mosses spring,
Underneath the tall oak's shadow,
Pretty, quiet, harmless thing,
Play about the sunny meadow.
Keep away from corn and house,
None will harm you, little mouse.

Cecil Frances Alexander

GREAT-GRANNY

IT'S lovely when Great-Granny comes,
  I watch for her for hours,
And jump for joy when she appears,
  With home-made jam, and flowers.

Today, she brought some marigolds,
  And in Mum's favourite jar,
They glow like little golden suns;
  How beautiful they are!

Mum always sets a dainty tea
  On cloth of creamy lace,
And Great-Gran praises everything,
  With happy, smiling face.

And afterwards, it's story time,
  I sit on Great-Gran's lap,
And have a cuddle, while Great-Gran
  Puts on her thinking-cap.

I've never seen her thinking-cap,
  But I feel sure it's blue,
With little frills around the edge,
  And ribbons threaded through.

Great-Granny's eighty-three years old,
  I'm very nearly four,
And every time she comes to tea
  I love her more and more!

Kathleen O'Farrell.

FIRST EDITIONS

MY library! Those priceless books
I cherish with such proud affection!
No wonder I'm on tenterhooks
Whenever any stranger looks
At my unique collection!
I fear lest he should wish to handle
Some volume from my shelves, the vandal!

The layman with unseeing eyes
Who tactlessly demands permission
To read them, cannot realise
How much those precious books I prize —
Each one a First Edition!
I turn deaf ears to all his pleading.
Such works were never meant for *reading*.

Ah, no! With true collector's care,
Like other First Edition lovers,
I keep my treasures hid somewhere,
All safely locked away in their
Original "dust covers",
Secreted in a private closet
Or stored within a Safe Deposit.

Yet, should your honesty be such
  That I can raise no real objection,
Or if I like you very much,
I'll let you view — you mustn't touch —
  Some gems from my collection,
And you'll appreciate my mania
For hoarding freakish miscellanea.

But though I'm lucky to have chanced
  On all these literary wonders
Whose market price has so advanced,
Whose value is so much enhanced
  By printers' happy blunders,
One thing I do deplore indeed:
I've not a single book to read!

Harry Graham

SEVEN TIMES ONE

THERE'S no dew left on the daisies and clover,
There's no rain left in heaven:
I've said my "seven times" over and over,
Seven times one are seven.

I am old, so old, I can write a letter;
My birthday letters are done;
The lambs play always, they know no better;
They are only one times one.

O moon, in the night I have seen you sailing
And shining so round and low;
You were bright, ah, bright, but your light is failing,
You are nothing now but a bow.

O velvet bee, you're a dusty fellow,
You've powdered your legs with gold!
O brave marsh marybuds, rich and yellow,
Give me your money to hold!

O columbine, open your folded wrapper,
Where two twin turtle-doves dwell!
O cuckoo-pint, toll me the purple clapper
That hangs in your clear green bell!

And show me your nest with the young ones in it;
I will not steal them away;
I am old! you may trust me, linnet, linnet —
I am seven times one today.

Jean Ingelow

AUTUMN ROOK

IN pensive mood at close of day
I watched rooks on their homeward way.
Each pair of wings was beating fast,
And as a lone, last straggler passed,
He called a harsh, ironic greeting.

Deep pools of shadow from the trees,
Like sable, still, mysterious seas,
Spread wider as the sun went down
To limn red-gold the valley town,
While dusk came, soft of foot and fleeting.

As up the quiet road I strolled,
Arose a breeze, unfriendly, cold;
And stars came out, remote and bright,
To hear the rumours of the night,
Their long, uncaring vigil keeping.

My thoughts returned to that sly bird
And to the mocking call I heard,
As to his resting place he sped,
Some leaf-bereft and breeze-tossed bed,
Fit for a feathered corsair's sleeping.

Peter Cliffe

LETTERS BETWEEN FRIENDS

WHEN I take a pen, dear friend,
And write a little note to you,
I try to picture where you are,
Your house and all the work you do.

I try to keep you in my heart,
As I relate the week now gone,
And you, as well, will visualise
My room with fire, and curtains drawn.

With fountain pen, I try to bring
Into your day a thought of home,
A little prayerful comforting,
For special needs that you've made known.

Letters twixt friends may often cheer
A very hard and trying day,
Make that loved someone very near,
As each to each their thoughts convey.

And so I pen a little verse,
And you will write a letter, too—
This is the way we may converse,
You, friend, with me — and I with you.

Margaret H. Dixon.

THE FALLOW DEER AT THE LONELY HOUSE

ONE without looks in tonight
  Through the curtain-chink
From the sheets of glistening white;
One without looks in tonight
  As we sit and think
  By the fender-brink.

We do not discern those eyes
  Watching in the snow;
Lit by lamps in rosy dyes
We do not discern those eyes
  Wondering, aglow,
  Fourfooted, tiptoe.

Thomas Hardy.

THE SKY

INFINITE space, serene and free,
  Blue in the clearness of the day;
Only a lone hawk hovers, still,
  Over the mountains far away.

Reaching for ever, unexplored,
  Into the fire of sunset's glow;
Cloud, and the mists, your secrets hide,
  Limits that we shall never know.

Only the moon that sails above,
  Only the clouds can know how far
Space may be stretching, past our flight,
  Reaching — beyond the utmost star.

Iris M. Raikes

The artists are:—

Charles Bannerman; The Garden, In Her Garden, Wishes For William, Point Of View, Family Life, Golden Hours, All Gone, Bookworm, Blue China.

Sheila Carmichael; A Spring Sonnet, A Malvern Lyric, Donegal Coast, Some Day, A Song Of Gloucestershire.

John Dugan; The House Of Winter Blossom, Rhyme Of The Rail, All The Gold, Harbour Lights, Ben, Would You Return?, Wine And Water, The Fallow Deer At The Lonely House.

Gilbert Dunlop; 'Mena, Where Is She Now?, An Old Woman Of The Roads.

Colin Gibson; Mountain Journey; Two Old Men.

Barbara Glebska; The Balliol Rooks, A Country Churchyard, The Fieldmouse, The Sky.

Alan Haldane; The Love Song, Last Of The Sails.

Harry MacGregor; On The Sussex Downs, On The River.

John Mackay; A Gipsy Life, The Weathercock, Planting Trees, The Voice, First Editions, Letters Between Friends.

Sandy Milligan; Beside Loch Eck, High Summer.

Douglas Phillips; Net Loss, Childhood Morning, Storm Warning, Great-Granny, Autumn Rook.

Staff Artists; The Way To Ericstane, Seven Times One.